GUIDE TO CHURCH USHERING

Second Revised Edition

HOMER J. R. ELFORD

Abingdon Press
Nashville

A GUIDE TO CHURCH USHERING (Revised)

Copyright © 1961 by Abingdon Press

Revised edition copyright © 1983 by Abingdon Press

New Second revised edition copyright © 1986 by Abingdon Press

Sixth Printing 1993

ISBN 0-687-16244-0
(Previously published under ISBN 0-687-16243-2)

MANUFACTURED IN THE UNITED STATES OF AMERICA

Church ushers share a religious heritage which dignifies their servant role. The Old Testament refers to them variously as "doorkeepers," "gatekeepers," and "keepers of the threshold" (I Chron. 16:38; Neh. 7:1; Esther 2:21; Jer. 35:4; Ps. 84:10*b*). Ezra listed them along with singers as "servants" who held official positions in temple worship (Ezra 2:70; 7:7).

Early Christian ushers not only welcomed worshipers, but sought to protect them from enemies. Today, ushers may feel a spiritual kinship to their early counterparts as they devote themselves to helping worshipers have a vibrant relationship with God.

The purpose of this book is to provide some practical suggestions for those who serve as church ushers.

Situations vary considerably, depending on traditions of denominations or local congregations, as well as particular circumstances. However, there are some fundamental principles that deserve consideration.

This book is dedicated to the loyal ushers who help make services of worship effective opportunities for experiencing the divine presence in places consecrated to God.

—HOMER J. R. ELFORD

CONTENTS

THE CHURCH USHER

Being a church usher is a sacred responsibility. It requires the same quality of dedication demanded of those who teach in the church school or sing in the choir. Very often the usher is the first person the worshiper meets when entering the church. First impressions are important. The attitude conveyed with words, facial expressions, and general deportment, as well as the appearance of the usher, will influence the worshiper. In a significant sense, it is a "public relations" position of the first order. Because the opportunity is so important, insofar as possible the usher should have no other duties in the church that might conceivably interfere with this work.

Spiritual Preparation

The church usher can radiate the very welcome of God to those who come to worship only if this feeling comes from the heart. This is not something that can be "put on" for the worship service as one dresses the body for the occasion. The usher must have a personal relationship with God through private and family daily devotions. Before the service let prayers be offered for God's guidance and inspiration in all that is said and done while serving in God's house. This sense of divine companionship will enable the usher to be sincere in greeting all who come, to "show hospitality to strangers," and to effectively meet any emergency that may arise.

A Sunday Morning Prayer

O God, I thank you for the opportunity to serve as one of your ministers today. May I be aware of your presence at all times as I welcome worshipers to your house. Enable me to be alert, courteous, and sensitive to their desires and needs. May all I do and say as an usher contribute to your honor and glory. Amen.

Physical Preparation

The church usher should be prepared physically to serve in this important office. We can be sure God does not expect all of us to be "fashion plates." The least we can do is to be well-groomed. Francis Bacon wrote, "Cleanness of body was ever deemed to proceed from a due reverence to God," and John Wesley used the phrase, "Cleanliness is indeed next to godliness."

The church ushering committee may choose to adopt some general, or even specific, rules about the clothes to be worn by the ushers so they may be dressed as uniformly as possible. Some churches warrant less formal clothing than others. Particular seasons of the year will undoubtedly determine the weight and perhaps the general color of attire. It is desirable, however, that some agreement be reached.

Some churches provide a flower or some type of badge to help identify the ushers. Boutonnieres are not worn at Communion services.

THE USHERING STAFF

Selection

T he selection of individuals to serve as church ushers varies considerably within different denominations and local churches. In some churches ushers are selected by the annual church meeting (session or quarterly conference). Sometimes they are appointed by the minister. Alas, in some churches they are just "collared" by some noble soul who has seen that a job ought to be done and hails the first persons who arrive on Sunday. In still other instances the church ushers are people who have done the job since time immemorial. No one remembers how they got the job, and in some cases no one is quite sure how to relieve them of their responsibility and open up the way for others to have a chance at this service to God.

It is better if the usher's term of office is on an annual selection basis. With this understanding no one should be offended when new persons are given the opportunity to serve.

It is preferred that, whenever possible, a number of people be considered for this important function, for it gives them an opportunity to share in the work of the church.

Some churches involve young people in the ushering program, often designating them "junior ushers." This praiseworthy policy deserves the same quality of selection, training, and discipline that is required for adult ushers.

Rotation

A rotation system provides a church with at least three times as many ushers as it may need on any particular occasion. In churches using this system, and where two or more services are held on a single day, the number would be sufficiently increased and would make it unnecessary for anyone to serve more than once a day, thus enlisting a larger corps of people. The outline of such a system appears on the following page.

It is desirable that church ushers be appointed or elected annually. Under the rotation system a chairperson is the principal officer. This should be someone with experience and ability as an organizational leader, someone who is capable of

Chairperson

July, October January, April	August, November February, May	September, December March, June
9:30 A.M.	9:30 A.M.	9:30 A.M.
Head Usher—	*Head Usher—*	*Head Usher—*
Ushers: Number needed for full complement	*Ushers:* Number needed for full complement	*Ushers:* Number needed for full complement
11:00 A.M.	11:00 A.M.	11:00 A.M.
Head Usher—	*Head Usher—*	*Head Usher—*
Ushers: Number needed for full complement	*Ushers:* Number needed for full complement	*Ushers:* Number needed for full complement
8:00 P.M.	8:00 P.M.	8:00 P.M.
Head Usher—	*Head Usher—*	*Head Usher—*
Ushers: Number needed for full complement	*Ushers:* Number needed for full complement	*Ushers:* Number needed for full complement

having general oversight of the total program of church ushering. He or she may have recently completed a term as a head usher.

The chairperson of the ushering committee, probably a former head usher, will be consulted by the chairperson of the nominating committee when head ushers are being chosen for nomination. They should be individuals in whom the chairperson has confidence and with whom all concerned can work creatively and harmoniously.

It shall be the duty of the chairperson of the ushering committee to call an organizational meeting immediately after elections (or appointments). At this meeting the head ushers, who come from the ranks of experienced ushers (while former head ushers, as well as the former chairperson, return to the ranks), will choose the people for their respective staffs. It is always well to do this in a meeting of all the ushers in order to ensure that the ushers agree to serve that particular "turn of duty" and that they understand they are to serve in the respective months outlined on the rotation chart.

After the initial organization the chairperson of the ushering committee should set up a training session to which all head ushers and church ushers come for instruction. It is also advisable that shorter review training sessions be held prior to each month's turn of duty for the respective corps of ushers.

The chairperson of the ushering committee will work closely with the minister in anticipation of the schedule of services, making sure that ushers are provided for all of them. Before the beginning of each month the chairperson of ushers and the minister will alert the head usher of all special services and those for which he or she will be responsible.

It is often advisable to check to see if the head usher is aware of the upcoming "turn of duty" again and if a full complement of ushers is available.

The chairperson of the ushering committee will be constantly alert to all matters pertaining to this work, making creatively critical suggestions to head ushers regarding the program and assuming the responsibility for filling in for any head usher in case of an emergency absence. Inasmuch as such special services as Holy Communion often require additional ushers, the chairperson will work with the head usher on duty that month in providing ushers for this service. The chairperson will also be responsible for providing ushers for church funerals.

At the organizational meeting the chairperson of the ushering committee will review the "rules" that have been adopted for ushering in their particular church. This is the proper time to remind all the ushering staff about the nature of their opportunity and responsibility, the expectations regarding punctuality and regularity, the times when they find it impossible to be present, the nature of deportment and clothes to be worn. In general, the material contained in this booklet, which should be given to all church ushers, should be reviewed and discussed in a question-and-answer period.

THE HEAD
USHER

The head usher is in charge of maintaining the ushering staff for all services at the appointed hour(s) during a particular month. (Note the chart.) The head usher should be at the church one hour (no later than forty-five minutes) *before* the service is scheduled to begin and should go over the checklist.

1. The entire staff of ushers is present.
2. An adequate supply of church bulletins is available for the ushers. It is important that the head usher see to it that ushers do not have to leave their assigned stations to replenish their supply of bulletins. For example, the head usher should know how many bulletins individual ushers, including balcony ushers, are likely to need and have these laid out when the usher arrives at his or her station.

3. Boutonnieres are laid out for the ushers. The head usher should take one.
4. The offering plates are where they should be.
5. The minister has been consulted regarding any unusual procedures to be followed in the service.

The head usher also checks with the custodian if something seems out of order—lights, ventilation, heat, doors locked that should be unlocked—and will be on the lookout for anything on the floor which could be hazardous, particularly on terrazzo, linoleum, or other polished surfaces. Paper clips, water, and other foreign materials can be dangerous.

This "official in charge" should be well acquainted with the location and the operation of such emergency equipment as fire extinguishers, wheelchairs, stretchers, and first-aid materials. All exits should be lighted and unlocked during the services.

The head usher strives to maintain "neatness" in the narthex and nave of the church. Often the opening of doorways causes the literature on the tables to become disheveled. Before each service of worship the pews should be cleared of used bulletins, hymnals (and prayer books) should be put in racks, and any "lost articles" should be taken to a place where they can be picked up by the owners.

The head usher should be alert to the seating position of doctors in order to summon them for telephone calls or for any emergencies that may arise.

If the nursery department has provided the head usher with information cards on which parents have written the name of their child and their own name, then he or she needs to note their seating position in order to summon them in case of emergency.

The head usher knows when doors leading from the narthex (foyer or entranceway) of the church into the nave (church proper) are to be closed or opened. (Note under "An Order of Service.") He or she will make clear to the ushers when people may be seated and will not permit the ushers to seat people except at those times.

The head usher remains in the narthex for a period extending from forty-five minutes before the service to the conclusion of the service and assumes the following responsibilities:

1. Greets worshipers at the outer door and directs them to ushers who have seats available.

2. Keeps alert to the location of available seats, seeking to maintain a balanced congregational seating arrangement.

3. Does not actually usher unless some post is vacant.

4. Seeks to maintain an atmosphere of reverent silence in the narthex, reminding the ushers that this is a service of worship, not a bazaar or an auction sale.

5. Greets, after the service has started, late-comers at the outer door and detains them in the narthex until the next designated opportunity for seating.

(Further duties of the head usher will be described under "An Order of Service.")

THE
USHER
AT WORK

Ushers who are to serve at a particular service should arrive at least a half hour prior to the service, or at a time agreed on by the ushering committee and designated by the chairperson and head usher.

If, for any reason, an usher cannot be present at the appointed time, he or she should notify the head usher in plenty of time for him or her to get a replacement.

The head usher provides each usher with a boutonniere, a supply of church bulletins, and, unless provided in the pew racks, prayer books and hymnals.

Now the usher takes the post of duty. This will probably be just inside the door leading from the narthex to the nave of the church, or at the beginning of the aisle which he or she is to serve.

It is imperative that the usher *stay* at the assigned post of duty, in readiness to serve the people who come to that door. People can be encouraged to wait at the door until the usher has returned from seating others. But "thou shalt not" go to the other side of the church to visit with a fellow usher. If the usher needs something, the head usher should be notified.

In churches where there are very long aisles, an usher may be stationed halfway to the front of the church. The first usher will then "feed" people to this second (or third) usher.

In some instances it is customary for the two or three ushers serving an aisle to work from this entranceway, taking their people to any seats available along their aisle.

It is desirable whenever possible for the ushers to know the people they guide to their seats and to know where they are accustomed to sitting. While folk should be encouraged to sit at various places in the church on different occasions to become acquainted with more of the worshipers, the fact is that many people prefer to sit in the same pew each Sunday. It should be understood that seats cannot be "held," particularly longer than fifteen minutes prior to the worship hour.

After a sincere greeting (not a noisy, boisterous, backslapping one, but one appropriate to the service of divine worship) and, if deemed necessary, a handshake and an inquiry as to where the person(s) would like to be seated, the usher then precedes the party at a reasonable gait (don't try to lead a relay race) down the aisle to the pew. If an unescorted woman is to be ushered by a man, it is proper for the usher to walk beside her, though the arm should not be offered or unnecessary conversation held.

One way to ensure that the people following the usher will continue to the appointed destination is for the usher to keep the bulletin in hand until they have arrived at the specified pew.

While it is sometimes difficult to avoid, because of the persistence of the people being ushered, no conversations should be engaged in by the usher on duty. It is disturbing to the other worshipers and distracts from the desired atmosphere of silence which should prevail in the house of the Lord. Certainly one must seek to avoid rudeness and must not be guilty of giving the impression that this is a "cold" church. The usher should give every token of cordial welcome, but talking—or even whispering—on the part of the ushers, either to worshipers or among themselves, is highly undesirable. This pertains to ushers in the narthex or to those waiting to serve in the aisles, as well as to those actually performing their service to people who have come to worship God (not to visit with people). Ushers have been known, as have so-called worshipers, to try to talk or whisper above the organ prelude. It cannot be overemphasized that the organ prelude is a definite part of the order of service. While seating may be done during this period, it should be done in the spirit of reverence. Some have even been heard to whisper during prayers or anthems or those periods when absolute silence should prevail. Ushers who persist in violating these rules should be replaced at the earliest possible occasion and certainly should not be reappointed to this sacred office.

AN
ORDER
OF SERVICE

An order of service is printed here to indicate the point in it when people may be seated.

While orders of service may vary, depending on the denomination and local situation, the principles outlined here can be adapted to particular circumstances.

ORDER OF WORSHIP

Morning Worship—Eleven O'clock

The head usher arrives no later than 10:15 A.M.—preferably at 10:00 A.M.; the ushers arrive at their posts of duty no later than 10:30—a half hour before the service.

Organ Prelude

Ushering may be done before and during this part of the service. Let it proceed as quietly as possible, for this is a time when worshipers are encouraged to enter into a period of silent prayer and meditation.

Spoken or Choral Call to Worship

The doors leading from the narthex into the nave of the church should be closed while the choir assembles. No one should be seated now until after the choir has begun the processional hymn. If no processional hymn is used, people still should not be seated until after the congregation has stood up for this opening hymn, and then they should be seated only from the side aisles. The doors from the narthex into the nave should be opened during the singing of the "Introit."

Processional Hymn or Opening Hymn

In those instances where the choir and clergy process down the center aisle, no one should be permitted to follow them until after they have entered the choir loft or chancel. This usually means that the center aisle should not be used during the service until those points marked with asterisks (****). Those arriving after the service of worship has begun may be seated during the singing of this opening hymn, but care should be taken that both the latecomer and the usher are out of the side aisle before the conclusion of the hymn and the beginning of the service.

Affirmation of Faith, Creed, Call to Worship
Let there be no seating of people during this part of the service. It is proper for the usher to provide these people who are held in the narthex with a bulletin so, with the usher, they may follow the service at this point. Let the attitude of worship prevail.

Gloria Patri
No seating.

Collect
No seating.

Lord's Prayer
No seating.

****Now is the time to seat those who have arrived in the narthex since the middle of the last verse of the opening hymn. It is highly desirable that the ushers strive to hold open a few seats near the rear of the auditorium and urge the latecomers to use these. It is preferable that those conducting the worship service not proceed with the service, except perhaps for announcements, until the latecomers have been seated and the ushers have returned to their stations. The organist should be encouraged to play some soft music at this interval.

Anthem
No seating.

****Again there is a time to seat those who have finally arrived.

Scripture Lesson

Choral or Spoken Invitation to Prayer
Silent Meditation

Pastoral Prayer
Choral or Spoken Amen

Offertory Sentences, Choral or Spoken
See chapter 6, "The Offering."

Offertory Anthem

Doxology

Hymn of Preparation
Latecomers may be seated near the rear.

Sermon

Hymn of Dedication

Benediction, Choral Response, Dismissal Chimes

Postlude

THE OFFERING

Receiving the offering is much more than "taking the collection." It is a time when the worshipers make a tangible acknowledgment of their conviction that God is the sovereign owner of all things and that they are stewards, and that God's ownership and their stewardship should be acknowledged through regular and systematic giving to Christ's church.

This being, therefore, an act of worship, those who perform the role of servants at this time are actually serving in that priestly office held by those who served in the temple as they presented "sacrifices" to the altar. The church usher is performing a very sacred office as he or she receives the offering and carries it to the minister who will lift it before the altar of the Most High. Therefore, the usher will proceed in an orderly and efficient manner.

At the appointed time the ushers should line up

in the back of the church and hold the empty offering plates in front of them with both hands.

At the prescribed signal from the head usher, probably aided by a certain musical note from the organ, they should all start together on the left foot. Practice should determine the stride to ensure that all the ushers arrive at the head of the aisles together. Let there be no racing, or any lagging. They are on the King's business!

In the order of service illustrated in chapter 5 the ushers leave the back of the church immediately at the conclusion of the choral amen, following the pastoral prayer. In some churches it is customary for the minister to make announcements just prior to the offering or to emphasize some particular financial appeal. In the church using the accompanying bulletin the announcements are made immediately following the first anthem, prior to the reading of the Scripture lesson. This issue should be made clear with the head usher and minister.

In most churches either a choral or spoken offertory sentence or prayer is made while the ushers are proceeding to the front of the church or before the receiving of the offering. If this is done the ushers will stand at their stations at the end of the front pews until the specified time. At the designated signal, probably after the offertory sentences of choral acknowledgment of steward-ship, the ushers turn and face the pew they are servicing and then pass the offering plate to the worshipers.

There should be an usher for each side of every section of pews. The usher in the center aisle passes the plate to those in the first pew; the usher in the side aisle passes the plate to the worshipers in the second pew, waiting there to receive the plate from the people of the first pew, then moving to the third pew, while the usher in the center aisle takes the plate from the end of the second pew and passes it to those sitting in the fourth pew. It is important also that the two ushers working a section wait for each other, lest two plates end up on the same aisle together.

Care should be taken that ushers keep in a reasonably straight line across the church.

In some churches ushers are asked to count people in the pews as they pass the offering plate and give the total to the head usher when they arrive at the back of the church.

The ushers who serve in the balcony are provided with offering plates at their stations, as are those who serve on the main floor. When the main floor ushers go to the front of the church to await the offertory sentences, the balcony ushers should stand at the front of the balcony rail, beginning their work when the main floor ushers begin. When they have completed receiving the offering from people in the balcony, these ushers should come forward, together, with the offering.

In the order of service in chapter 5 the ushers assemble in the narthex after taking the offering, give their seating totals to the head usher, and then proceed to line up, two abreast at each of three doors. The twelve ushers serving walk by twos down each of the three aisles. They await a signal from the head usher (who makes sure that the offertory anthem or organ offertory is completed and that all ushers are in readiness) and then proceed toward the front of the church, keeping in step and in line with ushers in the respective aisles. When they reach the chancel rail they assemble in a straight line in front of the minister(s). As the ushers have been approaching, the minister(s), choir, and congregation stand and sing the Doxology. While this is being sung the minister(s) collect(s) the offering plates and take(s) them to the altar. The ushers remain in their positions until the minister(s) turn(s) and step(s) away from the altar. Then the ushers make a quarter turn and move toward the center aisle, all proceeding to the narthex by way of the center aisle. This takes place, in this service, while the organist is playing the introduction to the hymn of preparation before the sermon.

THE USHER DURING THE SERMON

During the singing of the hymn of preparation all but two ushers, together with the head usher, should find places in the congregation. They may wish to join their families. It is highly important that the ushers who plan to join their families have them seated near the back of the church. In any case, they should not sit "down front," and should be in their chosen places before the conclusion of the hymn of preparation. In some churches a pew is reserved for them at the very back of the church.

Let the ushers not choose to "disappear." Some have been known to go to the church basement for a smoke; this is in poor taste. Ushers should be worshipers, even though their duty requires that they "work" in the "outer court of the Lord."

The head usher, and as many ushers as deemed necessary and designated, should remain in the narthex to greet latecomers and to care for any emergencies which may arise, such as calling doctors, notifying parents of a request for their presence in the nursery, and particularly being on hand in case of some situation that might endanger the worshipers or cause disturbance. (One Sunday a starling got into the basement of one church and some boys chased it out, quite unmindful of the desirability to be quiet. Alert ushers need to handle such situations with firmness.) It is highly important that the ushers on duty in the narthex during the sermon maintain absolute quiet. A loudspeaker usually provides them an opportunity to hear the sermon.

The head usher and the designated assistants will be prepared to open the doors leading from the nave to the narthex when the choir recesses or when the service has concluded. They will also open the street doors at the appropriate time—not before the close of the service for the noise and the elements may disturb the worshipers.

The head usher and assistants may assist the minister in greeting people as they leave the church. In some churches special "greeters" are appointed for this service. It is well to consider whether it is better to show this sign of hospitality after the service, rather than before. These "greeters" often interfere with the work of the ushers if they are on duty before the service.

SPECIAL SERVICES

The ushers who are serving during a prescribed month under the rotation system will serve, at the direction of their respective head usher, at special services during that month. As suggested in the rotation chart, if there are two or more corps of ushers serving at different services each Sunday, let it be determined by the chairperson of church ushering which corps will be responsible for a given special service. If it is deemed necessary, the head usher for this particular month, in consultation with the chairperson of church ushering, may solicit the help of others. It should be understood, however, that the head usher is responsible for special services, such as funerals, conferences, and rallies, which may be held during this month.

Holy Communion

The responsibilities of ushering at services of Holy Communion will, of course, depend on the practices of the denomination and the traditions of the local church.

Serving the elements in the pews. After the minister(s) has (have) partaken of the elements, all the ushers should proceed down the center aisles, or down their respective side aisles, as when preparing to receive the offering, lining up in front of the chancel rail.

The minister(s) will give plates of bread to those who are to serve in the balcony, allowing them to leave immediately to take places at the end of the front pews of the balcony. The minister(s) will then give a plate of bread to each of the main floor ushers. The number of ushers will depend on the number of people who are to be served. Inasmuch as the average tray for communion glasses will hold approximately forty glasses, ushers will be provided on that basis. This means that there is probably an usher for every five pews; two for every eight or ten. When all the ushers have been given plates of bread, the minister will give a signal for them to turn and go to their stations. Two ushers will go down each main aisle to a place no more than five pews from the rear; one usher will go down each outside aisle to that point. Perhaps two other ushers will go to within ten pews of the rear, two to a point fifteen pews from the rear, and so forth, making sure that the entire congregation is served. After the ushers arrive at their stations, they should await the action of the usher immediately in front of the minister, who will, in turn, await a signal from the minister indicating that all ushers are at their stations and that they may proceed.

The ushers will follow the same procedure as when passing the offering plates, facing the people in the pew they are serving, taking the plate at the end of the pew, and handing it to the people in the pew next to be served. When the designated number of worshipers have been served, the ushers take a piece of the bread in their hands, turn and face the altar, and await the word from the minister, "Take and eat this in remembrance that Christ died for you." Then the ushers join the other worshipers in partaking. At a given signal from the minister, or perhaps at the conclusion of a chime note by the organist, the leading usher will start forward on his or her left foot. The eyes of the other ushers whould be upon the leading usher so that they may start together. Proceeding to the front of the church, the ushers line up as before. The minister(s) receive(s) the plates which have been used and follow(s) the initial procedure, this time providing the ushers with trays of communion glasses. The same procedure is repeated. Many churches provide holders on the back of the pews for empty glasses. Otherwise they would have to be collected by the ushers (working from the back toward the front).

It is important that, as when receiving the offering, the ushers strive to keep in line with one another, even though those in some pews may pass the elements more slowly than others.

After the minister has received the used trays from the ushers there will be some whispered word of gratitude, which is their signal to turn and go to the rear of the church, just as they do at the appointed time after giving the minister the offering plates in the regular worship service.

When the ushers return to the narthex, they should maintain a reverent silence until the completion of this sacred service, preferably using their bulletin or prayer book to join in the ritual. While their duty puts some limitations on their getting the most out of services of worship, particularly Holy Communion, it need not keep them from benefiting from it entirely. This ideal can be promoted by their reverent attitude during this whole procedure and their participation in the ritual whenever possible.

Serving the elements at the chancel. The head usher will assign duties to the respective ushers. It is feasible to determine how many people can be served at the communion "table" at one time and then to indicate to the people how many may proceed at prescribed intervals.

At the prescribed time ushers proceed to the stations indicated by the head usher. This usually is to the ends of the front pews of each aisle. They then work "back" until all in that section have been served. It is sometimes customary to have a continual flow of people approaching the rail, so that as one "table" is dismissed, others may proceed to kneel. An usher should be stationed at the exit of the chancel to guide those who have communed away from the rail in another direction, thus avoiding a "traffic jam." In some places of worship it is considered advisable to have all the people approach the chancel from the extreme right side of the church. This often means that all will have to be directed from their pews to the rear of the church, across the back, and down that extreme left aisle of the church and down an aisle to their seats. This makes quite a trip for some people, and care should be taken to avoid confusion. Ushers wait until everyone else has been served before going as a group to the communion rail, probably after the choir has communed.

Particular customs and traditions in denominations and local congregations will undoubtedly determine the exact procedure during the administration of Holy Communion, but it is important that the ushers be alert and cooperate so that an orderly service is maintained.

Funerals

The chairperson of the ushering committee should clarify this issue in each particular church. Often the funeral director has a staff, which serves as ushers. It is helpful, however, that some well-informed member of the local church ushering staff be on hand to assist in the seating according to the direction of the funeral director. This layperson of the church of which the deceased was probably a member should make preparations for any emergencies that may arise.

The same reverent atmosphere of worship that we strive to attain in services of worship should exist at a funeral service. The presence of regular church ushers will help promote this ideal.

Weddings

Usually the ushers at a church wedding are friends who have been chosen by the bridegroom, so the church ushering staff has no responsibility.

Ushers at weddings should be at the wedding rehearsal to receive instructions from the minister.

While the bridal couple probably have some ideas of their own, it is well that these general rules be considered as basic for a well-ordered ceremony.

The ushers should arrive at the church at least a half hour before the ceremony. They should remember that this is a church and should conduct themselves in keeping with the sanctity of the place and the occasion.

At the rehearsal it will be decided what stations the respective ushers will fill. In a three-aisle church, two will serve the center aisle. At least one will serve each of the other aisles. The center aisle ushers will alternate in taking people down the aisle, usually serving a particular side of the aisle, that is, the bride's side and the groom's side, respectively. The groom's family and guests are seated on the right side of the church—right as one faces the altar from the rear; the bride's on the left. It is proper to have the women who are to be seated take the usher's arm. If the bride's guest is being seated, she will be on the usher's left arm walking near the pews, while the usher is on the side away from these pews. If she is the groom's guest, the woman should take the usher's right arm. The men follow along behind the usher and the woman. Each woman should be seated separately. Children will accompany their father, following their mother and the usher.

Pews to be reserved for members of the family should be designated at the rehearsal. The front pews on either side are reserved for the parents, and perhaps for other immediate members of the families of the bride and groom, respectively.

At the appointed time, the designated usher offers an arm to the mother of the groom and takes her to the front seat on the right where the father of the groom, and other immediate members of the family, have been seated previously. The father of the groom will arise and allow the mother of the groom to be seated; he then sits next to the aisle. After this usher has returned, the other center aisle usher escorts the mother of the bride to the front pew on the left. She leaves enough room for the father of the bride to be seated after he has given the bride away. Then this usher returns to the rear of the church.

The two center aisle ushers now march in step down to the chancel rail and pick up the ends of the white aisle cloth (crash) and unroll it.

If these ushers are to be at the front of the church for the wedding ceremony, then let them follow the direction of the minister with regard to getting there. In some churches, as soon as the organ chimes announce that the bride is ready, these ushers proceed down the right side aisle as the minister, bridegroom, and best man come from the vestry. The ushers fall in behind the best man at the chancel rail, facing toward the center aisle to await the bridesmaids.

After the ceremony is over, and the ushers have escorted the bride's attendants up the center aisle, the two center aisle ushers have another job to do.

The usher who escorted the bride's mother to her seat now proceeds down the aisle to the end of the pew in which the bride's family is seated. Let him touch the father of the bride on the shoulder to indicate that he is to stand and face the usher—facing toward the rear of the church. The mother of the bride now arises and takes the arm of the usher who has, in the meantime, turned toward the rear of the church. With her on his right arm, the usher escorts her to the narthex of the church, the father of the bride following behind them.

When the bride's parents have been escorted to the narthex, the other center aisle usher follows the same procedure, using his left arm to escort the groom's mother to the narthex.

Now these two ushers march up the center aisle together, taking their stations at the end of the first pew that is occupied. The usher on the bride's side bows to the people in the first occupied pew, indicating that they may go out; he does not escort them out. After those in that first pew on the bride's side have started up the aisle, the usher on the groom's side bows out those on his side, the ushers alternating until all pews have been emptied.

The other ushers direct people to the reception line or room.

It should be made clear at the rehearsal who is to light the candles, and at what time. In most churches these are lighted half an hour prior to the ceremony, often by the ushers who service the side aisles.

The wedding ushers, like regular church ushers, should know about the facilities of the church and the location of emergency equipment.

GREETERS

In many churches specified persons serve as greeters. This is a good custom, for greeters convey hospitality to visitors, but some guidelines and disciplines should be established for them by the Worship Committee.

The selection and rotation systems used for ushers, outlined in chapter 2, may also prove helpful for greeters.

When greeters serve, they should not get in the way, usurp, or hinder the work of the ushers.

They should observe the same spiritual and physical preparations, as well as the disciplines, as ushers do, because they are welcoming people who are entering the church to worship. This purpose deserves respect.

Greeters should be persons who recognize "strangers" immediately and act accordingly—welcoming them, urging them to sign the register, and sometimes providing them with a ribbon or